HOW SAFE IS YOUR MOTORCYCLE ?

An MOT handbook on mechanical safety

LONDON: HMSO

Written and Designed by
Nick Lynch and Jon Starte

COMIND
Cambridge

First Published 1989
Second impression 1990

ISBN 0 11 550911 9

Foreword

A good rider deserves a good machine. That means one that is properly equipped and maintained. The standard needed to pass an MOT test is the minimum standard needed to ride lawfully on a road at any time, not forgetting that the noise levels of your machine must conform to the law. It is also the standard which, coupled with your skill as a rider, can make all the difference between life and death when you are out on the open road.

The series of practical regular checks set out in this book are a handy way to make sure you have not forgotten anything. Safe riding.

Robert Atkins MP
Minister for Roads and Traffic

INTRODUCTION

Why motorcyclists should use this book

This book is produced by the Vehicle Inspectorate Executive Agency and sponsored by Norwich Union Insurance. Its purpose is to give motorcyclists easy to follow advice on how to keep their bikes safe, in good condition and within the legal requirements of the "MOT" Test.

It is not intended to interpret the law governing the "MOT" Test: that's a matter for the courts to determine.

This book does not replace the existing official MOT Inspection Manual "Motor Cycle Testing" used in the Test and also available from HMSO. Some testable items, such as brakes and headlamp-beam aim, can be difficult for you to check effectively without proper equipment.

This means that your motorcycle can still fail, although you might have followed the procedures in this book to the letter. Remember that the MOT tester is specially trained and experienced: pass or fail is at his discretion.

If you feel you have a genuine grievance over a failure, you can appeal to the Vehicle Inspectorate's District Office (see page 52).

While this book has been put together as a manual for those who want to check and/or prepare their motorcycle for the "MOT" Test, it makes good sense to follow regularly the routines set out. Even if your bike is not due for an "MOT" Test, or perhaps not even within the scope of the scheme, it will pay you to carry out all these checks as part of your routine maintenance.

Put right any defects straight away: a minor defect can become dangerous if you neglect it.

If you have any doubts, don't hesitate to seek expert advice.

CONTENTS

FOLLOW THESE STEPS TO CHECK
YOUR MOTORCYCLE

Ensure your motorcycle is clean because testers can refuse to test dirty bikes
(It also makes good sense to keep your motorcycle as clean as possible at all times)

Start

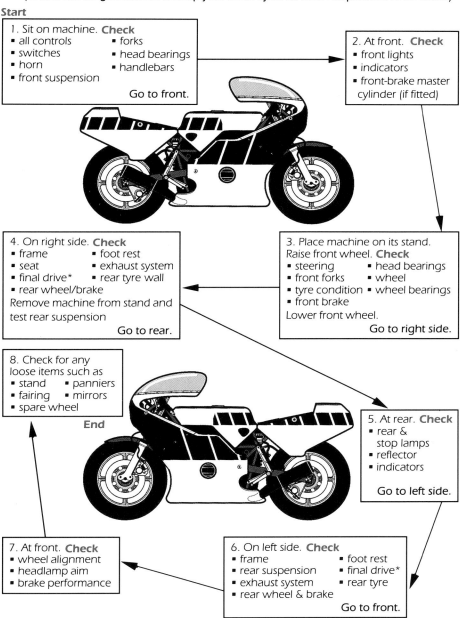

1. Sit on machine. **Check**
- all controls
- switches
- horn
- front suspension
- forks
- head bearings
- handlebars

Go to front.

2. At front. **Check**
- front lights
- indicators
- front-brake master cylinder (if fitted)

4. On right side. **Check**
- frame
- seat
- final drive*
- rear wheel/brake
- foot rest
- exhaust system
- rear tyre wall

Remove machine from stand and test rear suspension

Go to rear.

3. Place machine on its stand. Raise front wheel. **Check**
- steering
- front forks
- tyre condition
- front brake
- head bearings
- wheel
- wheel bearings

Lower front wheel.

Go to right side.

8. Check for any loose items such as
- stand
- fairing
- spare wheel
- panniers
- mirrors

End

5. At rear. **Check**
- rear & stop lamps
- reflector
- indicators

Go to left side.

7. At front. **Check**
- wheel alignment
- headlamp aim
- brake performance

6. On left side. **Check**
- frame
- rear suspension
- exhaust system
- rear wheel & brake
- foot rest
- final drive*
- rear tyre

Go to front.

*Final drive may be fitted to the left or right of the rear wheel.

1

LIGHTS - 1

Are your front lights safe ?

WHAT THE MOT REQUIRES	YOUR LIGHTS WHAT TO CHECK
The Front Lights **Your motorcycle must have:** 1. A front position lamp (if the machine has no headlamp) 2. A dipped-beam headlamp 3. A main-beam headlamp 4. A front position lamp on the sidecar if a motorcycle combination is being used Position lamps must give out white light unless incorporated in a head-lamp with a yellow lens These lamps • must be clean and in good working order. • must show a steady light Motorcycles used only in daylight do not require lamps. You must either remove **all** lamps or disconnect and mask them Motorcycles first registered before 1 Jan 1972 with an engine capacity of less than 50cc, or which cannot exceed 25mph, require only a dipped beam headlamp	**Turn on lights and make sure that:** a. all lamps show an uninterrupted and steady white or yellow light visible from a reasonable distance b. the light of any lamp is not affected when you switch on another lamp c. no lamp flickers when tapped d. each lamp is secure e. no lens is damaged or missing f. all switches work correctly

DIAGRAM SHOWING FRONT LAMP

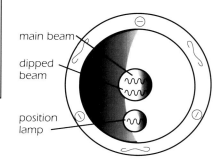

main beam

dipped beam

position lamp

2

Are your front lights safe ?

MAIN REASONS FOR FAILURE	REMARKS	ACTION	✓
1. No front lamp showing an uninterrupted and steady WHITE or YELLOW light visible from a reasonable distance	⚠ ⚠ ⚠	Check lamp Repair wiring/ Replace Recharge battery	
2. A lamp which • does not light up as soon as it is switched on • is affected by the working of another lamp • flickers when you tap it	⚠ ⚠ ⚠	Check wiring and connections	
3. A lens which is • missing • damaged	⚠	Repair/Replace	
4. An unsecured lamp	⚠ ⚠	Tighten	
5. A faulty switch	⚠ ⚠	Repair/Replace	

WARNING

⚠ ⚠ ⚠ Extremely dangerous. DO NOT ride your motorcycle in this condition.

You will be breaking the law and risking your life and the lives of others.

 Very dangerous. Put right immediately.

 Could also be dangerous.

LIGHTS - 3

HOW TO TEST YOUR LIGHTS

Things you will need:
A wall (such as the garage wall)
A helpful friend
A piece of chalk or other suitable marker

a. Check that the tyres are correctly inflated and the motorcycle is on level ground.

b. Draw on the wall
- a horizontal line about 1m long and at the same height as the headlamp lens centre
- a vertical line about 1m long forming a cross with the horizontal line

c. Position the motorcycle so that
- it squarely faces the wall
- the steering is straight and the front wheel is pointing at the cross
- the headlamp lens is 3.8 metres (12.5ft) from the wall

d. With a friend sitting on the motorcycle in the normal driving position whilst holding it upright, switch on the headlamps 'main' and 'dipped' beams in turn. One of the beams will match one of the three images shown diagrammatically below.

e. Check that the boundaries of the beam image are not outside the limits given in the appropriate diagram

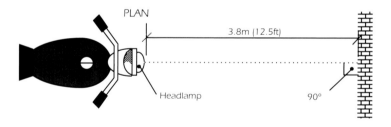

HEADLAMPS CHECKED ON MAIN (DRIVING) BEAM

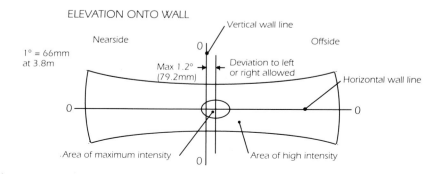

LIGHTS - 4

HEADLAMPS CHECKED ON EUROPEAN TYPE DIPPED BEAM

ELEVATION ONTO WALL

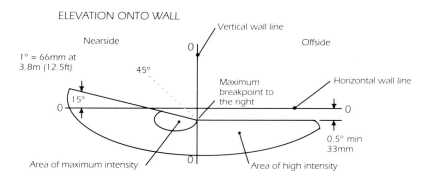

ELEVATION TO MOTORCYCLE

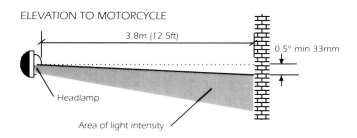

HEADLAMPS CHECKED ON BRITISH AMERICAN TYPE DIPPED BEAM

ELEVATION ONTO WALL

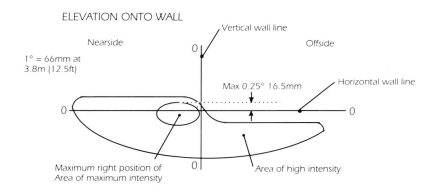

LIGHTS - 5

WHAT THE MOT REQUIRES	HOW TO CHECK YOUR LIGHTS
The Rear Lights **Your motorcycle must have:** 1. A **rear position lamp** which gives out a RED light (motorcycle/sidecar combinations must have two) 2. A **stop lamp** which gives out a steady red light when you apply the brakes These lamps must be clean and in good working order The rear position lamp must show a steady red light Motorcycles used only in daylight do not require lamps. You must either remove **all** lamps or disconnect and mask them Motorcycles first registered after 1 April 1986 must have a stop lamp which is activated by BOTH the front and back braking systems Motorcycles not required to have a stop lamp are those • first used before 1 Jan 1986 with an engine capacity of less than 50cc, and/or • with a maximum speed not exceeding 25mph	**Turn on lights and make sure that** a. the rear position lamp shows a steady RED light b. when the brakes are applied the RED stop lamp lights up c. no lamp is affected by the operation of any other lamp d. no lamp flickers when tapped e. each lamp is secure f. no lens is damaged or missing g. all switches work correctly

Your stop lamp may be the ONLY warning you give drivers behind that you are stopping. A faulty stop lamp could mean NO stop lamp !

Are your rear lights safe ?

MAIN REASONS FOR FAILURE	REMARKS	ACTION	✓
1. The stop lamp does not show a red light when you apply the brakes	⚠ ⚠	Check lamp Check wiring Repair/Replace	
2. A stop lamp which does not stay steadily lit while you keep the brakes applied	⚠ ⚠	Check wiring Repair/Replace	
3. The stop lamp remains on while the brakes are not being applied	⚠	Check wiring Repair/Replace	
4. A rear position lamp which does not show a steady red light	⚠ ⚠	Check wiring Repair/Replace	
5. A stop or rear position lamp which • does not light up as soon as it is switched on • is affected by the working of another lamp • flickers when you tap it	⚠ ⚠	Check wiring Repair/Replace	
6. A lens is • missing • damaged	⚠	Replace	
7. An unsecured lamp	⚠ ⚠	Tighten	
8. A faulty switch	⚠ ⚠	Repair/Replace	

WARNING

 Very dangerous. Put right immediately.

⚠ Could also be dangerous.

LIGHTS - 7

Are your indicators working properly ?

WHAT THE MOT REQUIRES	HOW TO CHECK YOUR INDICATORS
The Indicators **Your motorcycle must have direction indicators which** • show an amber light (if the machine was first used on or after 1 September 1965) • flash 60-120 times per minute (with the engine idling if necessary) • can be seen by the rider from a normal riding position (if not an audible or visible telltale must be fitted) • are clean and in good working order **Motorcycles and combinations NOT required to have direction indicators are those** • first used before 1 April 1986 • with a maximum speed not exceeding 25mph • made for off-road use • which have no other lamps	**Turn on direction indicators in turn and make sure that** a. the light is amber colour b. they flash 60-120 times a minute c. the intensity is reasonable d. the telltale is working correctly if the indicators are not visible from the riding position e. no lamp affects the working of any other lamp f. no lamp flickers when tapped g. each lamp is secure h. no lens is damaged or missing i. the switches work correctly

8

Are your indicators working properly ?

MAIN REASONS FOR FAILURE	REMARKS	ACTION	✓
1. An indicator is missing or can't be seen	⚠ ⚠	Repair/Replace	
2. An indicator is • not showing an amber light • not visible from a reasonable distance	⚠ ⚠	Check wiring Repair/Replace	
3. An indicator which is • not working • not flashing at the correct rate • affected by another lamp	⚠ ⚠	Check wiring Repair/Replace	
4. A light which • does not light up as soon as it is switched on • is affected by the working of another lamp • flickers when you tap it	⚠ ⚠	Check wiring Repair/Replace	
5. A lens which is • missing • damaged • not doing its job	⚠	Repair/Replace	
6. An unsecured lamp	⚠ ⚠	Tighten	
7. A faulty switch	⚠	Repair/Replace	

WARNING

 Very dangerous. Put right immediately.

⚠ Could also be dangerous.

LIGHTS - 9

Are your reflectors in good condition ?

WHAT THE MOT REQUIRES	HOW TO CHECK YOUR REFLECTOR
The rear reflector **Your motorcycle must have :** 1. A **rear reflex reflector** (combinations must have two) which ▪ is aligned vertically and faced squarely to the rear ▪ must be clean Machines used only during the day which have no lamps, or have masked and disconnected lamps, need not have a reflector Extra reflectors will not be tested **NOTE: Reflective tape is NOT an acceptable substitute for a reflector**	**Check you have a clean RED rear reflector** a. Examine its condition and security

10

LIGHTS - 10

Are your reflectors in good condition ?

MAIN REASONS FOR FAILURE	REMARKS	ACTION	✓
1. A rear reflector is missing or obscured		Repair/Replace	
2. A reflector is • damaged • not doing its job		Repair/Replace	
3. An unsecure reflector		Tighten	

WARNING

 Could be dangerous.

STEERING - 1

Is your motorcycle's steering safe ?

WHAT THE MOT REQUIRES	HOW TO CHECK YOUR STEERING
The Steering Controls The condition of the STEERING must not cause danger to any person on the motorcycle or on the road The STEERING must be in good and efficient working order and be properly adjusted	**How to check your steering** a. With the wheels supporting the motorcycle on the ground, grasp the handle bars tightly and check for • loose grips • loose clamps • weak handlebars or fork yokes b. With the front wheels off the ground check that • there is nothing interfering with the controls • when you turn the handlebars the grips do not come too close to any other part of the motorcycle • when on full lock the cables are not taut or likely to get trapped • any steering damper is fitted correctly c. Check that steering lock stops are fitted correctly

Is your motorcycle's steering safe ?

MAIN REASONS FOR FAILURE	REMARKS	ACTION	✓
1. Handlebar clamps are not tight or bolts are loose or missing	⚠ ⚠ ⚠	Tighten/Replace	
2. Handlebar or fork yoke is • fractured • cracked • excessively corroded	⚠ ⚠ ⚠	Replace	
3. Any part of the motorcycle interferes with the free movement of the handlebars from lock to lock	⚠ ⚠ ⚠	Tighten/Replace	
4. Loose handgrips	⚠ ⚠ ⚠	Tighten/Replace	
5. Taut or trapped cables	⚠ ⚠	Repair/Replace	
6. Insufficient clearance between grips and part of the machine on full lock	⚠ ⚠	Check stops	
7. An insecure steering damper or ineffective steering damper	⚠ ⚠ ⚠	Tighten Replace	
8. An insecure fairing or leg shield or one which can interfere with the steering	⚠ ⚠	Tighten/Relocate	
9. A flexible handlebar mounting which is very deteriorated or a rigid handlebar which is deformed	⚠ ⚠	Replace	
10. A steering lock stop which is • missing • not adjusted properly • loose	⚠	Tighten/Adjust/ Replace	

WARNING

⚠ ⚠ ⚠ Extremely dangerous. DO NOT ride your motorcycle in this condition.

You will be breaking the law and risking your life and the lives of others.

⚠ ⚠ Very dangerous. Put right immediately.

⚠ Could also be dangerous.

13

STEERING - 3

Is your motorcycle's steering safe ?

WHAT THE MOT REQUIRES	HOW TO CHECK YOUR STEERING
The Steering System The condition of the STEERING must not cause danger to any person on the motorcycle or on the road The STEERING must be in good and efficient working order and be correctly adjusted	**Is your steering system in good condition ?** Check that the head bearings are correctly adjusted so that with the front brake applied there is no ■ free play when the machine is rocked forward and backward, or ■ roughness or binding when the handlebars are turned from lock to lock

STEERING - 4

Is your motorcycle's steering safe ?

MAIN REASONS FOR FAILURE	REMARKS	ACTION	✓
1. Steering movement is excessively stiff, 'notchy', or rough	⚠ ⚠ ⚠	Adjust/Replace	
2. Too much free play in head bearings	⚠ ⚠ ⚠	Adjust/Replace	

WARNING

 Extremely dangerous. DO NOT ride your motorcycle in this condition.

You will be breaking the law and risking your life and the lives of others.

SUSPENSION & WHEEL BEARINGS - 1

Is your motorcycle's suspension in good condition ?

WHAT THE MOT REQUIRES	HOW TO CHECK YOUR SUSPENSION
The Front Suspension The condition of the SUSPENSION must not cause danger to any person on the motorcycle or on the road The SUSPENSION must be maintained in good and efficient working order and be properly adjusted	**How to check the condition of your front suspension** a. Check the condition, alignment and security of the front fork assembly b. Check wear in front forks ▪ With the front wheel between your knees try to move the handlebars from side to side to check for free play ▪ On leading or trailing-link suspensions try to move the swinging fork from side to side to check for free play c. With the front wheel raised, check the wheel bearings are not too tight or too loose and spin the wheel to listen for roughness d. With the front wheel on the ground apply front brake and depress the forks to ensure freedom of movement and effectiveness of damping e. Check the front mudguard is in good condition, secure and not touching other parts of the machine

SUSPENSION & WHEEL BEARINGS - 2

Is your motorcycle's suspension in good condition ?

MAIN REASONS FOR FAILURE	REMARKS	ACTION	✓
1. A fork assembly component which is • loose • cracked • very bent • corroded • not correctly aligned	⚠⚠⚠	Adjust/Replace	
2. A broken spring	⚠⚠⚠	Replace	
3. An oil leak showing damper seal failure	⚠	Replace	
4. Too much free play between sliding parts of the forks or pivot bearings	⚠ ⚠	Adjust/Replace	
5. Loose • wheel spindle • securing nuts • locking device	⚠⚠⚠	Tighten/Lock	
6. Wheel bearings which are too tight or too loose	⚠ ⚠	Adjust	
7. Bearings which feel rough	⚠	Replace	
8. A fault which might prevent the forks operating freely	⚠ ⚠	Repair/Replace	
9. The forks are too stiff	⚠	Repair/Replace	
10. A loose mudguard or one that could contact • the wheel • the tyre • any fixed part of the machine	⚠⚠⚠	Tighten/Replace	
11. A shock absorber with not enough damping	⚠ ⚠	Replace	

WARNING

 Extremely dangerous. DO NOT ride your motorcycle in this condition.

You will be breaking the law and risking your life and the lives of others.

 Very dangerous. Put right immediately.

Could also be dangerous.

17

SUSPENSION & WHEEL BEARINGS - 3

Is your motorcycle's suspension in good condition ?

WHAT THE MOT REQUIRES	HOW TO CHECK YOUR SUSPENSION
The Rear Suspension The condition of the SUSPENSION must not cause danger to any person on the motorcycle or on the road The SUSPENSION must be in good and efficient working order and be correctly adjusted	**How to check the condition of your rear suspension** a. Check the condition, alignment and security of the rear suspension components b. With the rear wheel raised, check the wheel bearings are not too tight or too loose and spin the wheel to listen for roughness c. Check for play in the suspension bearings by moving the suspension from side to side d. Sit on seat and depress rear suspension several times and check for • freedom of movement • effectiveness of damping

SUSPENSION & WHEEL BEARINGS - 4

Is your motorcycle's suspension in good condition ?

MAIN REASONS FOR FAILURE	REMARKS	ACTION	✔
1. A suspension component which is • loose • cracked • very bent • not correctly aligned • corroded	⚠️⚠️⚠️	Adjust/Replace	
2. A broken spring	⚠️⚠️⚠️	Replace	
3. An oil leak showing damper seal failure	⚠️	Replace	
4. Too much free play or deterioration in a suspension joint	⚠️⚠️	Adjust/Replace	
5. Loose • wheel spindle • securing nuts • locking device	⚠️⚠️⚠️	Tighten/Lock	
6. Wheel bearings which are too tight or too loose	⚠️⚠️	Adjust	
7. Bearings which feel rough	⚠️	Replace	
8. A fault which might hinder the moving parts of the suspension	⚠️⚠️	Repair/Replace	
9. The suspension is too stiff	⚠️	Repair/Replace	
10. A shock absorber with not enough damping	⚠️⚠️	Replace	

WARNING

 Extremely dangerous. DO NOT ride your motorcycle in this condition.

You will be breaking the law and risking your life and the lives of others.

 Very dangerous. Put right immediately.

⚠️ Could also be dangerous.

WHEEL ALIGNMENT - 1

Are your wheels correctly aligned ?

WHAT THE MOT REQUIRES	HOW TO CHECK YOUR ALIGNMENT
The Wheel Alignment The ALIGNMENT of the wheels must be correct and must not cause danger to any person on the motorcycle or on the road	**How to check the alignment of your wheels** a. Clamp the wheel or ask a friend to help you ensure the front wheel is held upright and in line with the frame with the machine off its stand • Using a straight edge or piece of cord against the rear wheel check the two wheels are in line. Repeat this on the opposite side and ensure that alignment is correct • Look along the front wheel and forks and check for correct alignment

Plan of wheel alignment positions for equal size tyres

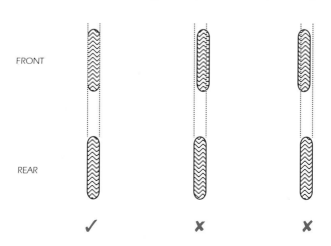

FRONT

REAR

✓   ✗   ✗

WHEEL ALIGNMENT - 2

Are your wheels correctly aligned ?

MAIN REASONS FOR FAILURE	REMARKS	ACTION	✓
1. Any misalignment likely to affect the handling or steering of the machine		Align correctly, replace as necessary	

WARNING

 Very dangerous. Put right immediately.

Plan of wheel alignment positions for wide rear tyres

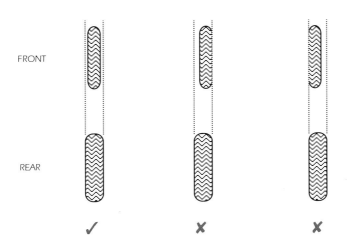

FRONT

REAR

✓   ✗   ✗

21

BRAKES - 1

Do the brake controls work properly ?

WHAT THE MOT REQUIRES	HOW TO CHECK YOUR BRAKES
The Brake Controls The condition of the BRAKES must not cause danger to any person on the motorcycle or on the road The BRAKES must be in good and efficient working order and be correctly adjusted Motorcycles registered on or after 1 January 1927 must have • two efficient braking systems, with separate controls, or • one system with two separate controls The application of one brake must not affect the working of the other	**How to check your brake controls** a. Check that the required braking systems are fitted b. Check the condition and security of the • pedal • handlebar brake lever • mountings c. Fully operate the brake pedal and lever several times and look for • security • wear at pivots • reserve travel • the position of the pedal or lever in relation to the foot rest or handlebar • smoothness d. In an hydraulic system, apply the control hard and check for 'creep' and 'sponginess'

Do the brake controls work properly ?

MAIN REASONS FOR FAILURE	REMARKS	ACTION	✓
1. The motorcycle does not have the required braking systems	⚠ ⚠	Replace	
2. The brake lever or mounting is • loose • cracked or the attachment screws are • loose • missing	⚠ ⚠ ⚠	Tighten/Replace	
3. A control lever cannot be fully or properly applied	⚠ ⚠ ⚠	Repair/Replace	
4. Lever pivots are badly worn	⚠ ⚠	Replace	
5. A control which is • positioned • bent • shortened so that the brake cannot be readily applied	⚠ ⚠	Repair/Replace	
6. Inadequate reserve travel of lever	⚠ ⚠ ⚠	Check wear/ Adjust	
7. A control not working smoothly	⚠	Repair/Replace	
8. A hydraulic system which • creeps* • is spongy*	⚠ ⚠ ⚠	Repair/Replace	

WARNING

⚠ ⚠ ⚠ Extremely dangerous. DO NOT ride your motorcycle in this condition.

You will be breaking the law and risking your life and the lives of others.

 Very dangerous. Put right immediately.

 Could also be dangerous.

* Creep is when, under constant pressure, a lever or pedal moves slowly
* If there is air in the system, the brakes will feel 'spongy' when applied and there may be excessive travel

BRAKES - 3

WHAT THE MOT REQUIRES	HOW TO CHECK YOUR BRAKES
The Brake System	**MECHANICAL BRAKE COMPONENTS**
The condition of the BRAKES must not cause danger to any person on the motorcycle or on the road	Examine all the mechanical parts you can see, without dismantling, looking for
The BRAKES must be in good and efficient working order and be correctly adjusted	a. General
Motorcycles registered on or after 1 January 1927 must have	• corrosion • insecurity • cracking • restrictions to free movement • abnormal movement • too much wear (especially to pads/linings) • incorrect adjustment
• two efficient braking systems, with separate controls, or	b. Cables, rods, levers, links which are
• one system with two separate controls	• badly chafed • damaged • frayed or knotted cables • worn clevis joint • missing or loose locking devices
The application of one brake must not affect the working of the other	c. Calipers, backplates, drums and discs which are
	• insecure (including reaction brackets) • greasy or oily • scored, pitted • worn • distorted

IN FRONT

Norwich Union have been the market leader for motorcycle insurance for almost twenty years. They insure more than six out of every ten riders. Have you ever wondered why?

NORWICH
UNION

ALONGSIDE

Norwich Union introduced their "Rider" policy in 1969. It revolutionised motor cycle insurance by covering the policyholder to ride any bike, including friends' bikes, up to a selected c.c. limit. This approach, and the simplified proposal are as popular today as they were twenty years ago. And Norwich Union's extensive branch network means they can offer a truly local service. So important when it comes to settling claims.

Norwich Union. Getting alongside their customers by identifying their particular needs.

NORWICH
UNION

B E H I N D

Norwich Union, as a caring insurer, offer their customers more than just a first class service. Their other activities reflect their concern for safety. Like sponsoring the Highway Code video. And mailing their policyholders road safety leaflets. Even the sponsorship of this publication!

Norwich Union. Committed to road safety, and behind you all the way.

BRAKES - 4

Does the brake system work properly ?

MAIN REASONS FOR FAILURE	REMARKS	ACTION	✓
1. Serious weakening of any component due to • cracking • too much wear • damage (eg reduction of brake rod by 1/3rd of original diameter)	⚠ ⚠ ⚠	Replace	
2. A cable which is • corroded • knotted • frayed • damaged outer casing	⚠ ⚠ ⚠ ⚠ ⚠	Replace	
3. A badly worn clevis joint	⚠ ⚠	Replace	
4. Insecure or missing locking devices (eg lock nuts, split pins)	⚠ ⚠	Tighten/Replace	
5. Brake linings or pads less than manufacturers recommended minimum or1.5mm thick at any point	⚠	Replace	
6. Missing, insecure or cracked • brake drum • disc • securing bolts	⚠ ⚠ ⚠	Tighten/Replace	
7. Any restriction to the free movement of the system	⚠ ⚠ ⚠	Repair	
8. Abnormal movement of levers indicating maladjustment or excessive wear	⚠ ⚠ ⚠	Adjust/Replace	
9. Missing, insecure or cracked • brake back plate • reaction bracket • caliper • securing bolt	⚠ ⚠ ⚠	Repair/Replace	
10. A disc which is • distorted • oily or greasy • pitted • worn • scored	⚠ ⚠ ⚠ ⚠	Clean/Repair/ Replace	

WARNING

 Extremely dangerous. DO NOT ride your motorcycle in this condition.

You will be breaking the law and risking your life and the lives of others.

 Very dangerous. Put right immediately.

⚠ Could also be dangerous.

BRAKES - 5

WHAT THE MOT REQUIRES	HOW TO CHECK YOUR BRAKES
The Brake System The condition of the BRAKES must not cause danger to any person on the motorcycle or on the road The BRAKES must be in good and efficient working order and be correctly adjusted Motorcycles registered on or after 1 January 1927 must have • two efficient braking systems, with separate controls, or • one system with two separate controls The application of one brake must not affect the working of the other	**HYDRAULIC BRAKE COMPONENTS** a. Examine hydraulic reservoirs and cylinders and check for • security of mounting • corrosion • damage • presence of reservoir cap • fluid level • leaks b. Examine all visible brake pipes and flexible hoses for • chafing • corrosion • damage • security • fouling • leaks • kinking • stretching c. Apply the brakes firmly and check for • leaks • bulges in hoses

Does the brake system work properly ?

MAIN REASONS FOR FAILURE	REMARKS	ACTION	✓
1. A reservoir or cylinder is • insecurely mounted • corroded • damaged	⚠ ⚠ ⚠ ⚠ ⚠	Repair/Replace	
2. Reservoir cap is missing	⚠ ⚠ ⚠	Drain and refill system and replace cap	
3. Dangerously low fluid level	⚠ ⚠ ⚠	Fill up/Investigate	
4. Any leak of hydraulic fluid	⚠ ⚠ ⚠	Repair/Replace	
5. Pipes that are • chafed • corroded • damaged • cracked • inadequately supported if rigid • likely to hinder or be trapped by moving parts	⚠ ⚠ ⚠	Repair/Replace	
6. Hoses that are • damaged • chafed • deteriorated • cracked • bulging under pressure • stretched by steering or suspension • likely to hinder or be trapped by moving parts	⚠ ⚠ ⚠	Replace	

WARNING

⚠ ⚠ ⚠ Extremely dangerous. DO NOT ride your motorcycle in this condition.

You will be breaking the law and risking your life and the lives of others.

⚠ ⚠ Very dangerous. Put right immediately.

27

BRAKES - 7

Are your brakes working correctly ?

WHAT THE MOT REQUIRES	HOW TO CHECK YOUR BRAKES
The Brake System The condition of the BRAKES must not cause danger to any person on the motorcycle or on the road The BRAKES must be in good and efficient working order and be correctly adjusted Motorcycles registered on or after 1 January 1927 must have • two efficient braking systems, with separate controls, or • one system with two separate controls The application of one brake must not affect the working of the other A motorcycle or motorcycle combination must have a braking efficency of not less than 30% by one brake system and 25% by the other	**How to check your brake PERFORMANCE** Ride the motorcycle and apply the brakes firmly with constant pressure. They should work • progressively • without juddering • without fluctuation Note. The Tester will use a stringent test, so make sure the brakes are working correctly

Do your brakes work correctly ?

MAIN REASONS FOR FAILURE	REMARKS	ACTION	✓
1. There is an efficiency of less than 30% when one of the brakes is applied*	⚠ ⚠ ⚠	Repair/Adjust/ Replace	
2. There is an efficiency of less than 25% when the other is applied*	⚠ ⚠ ⚠	Repair/Adjust/ Replace	
3. A brake is sticking or binding	⚠ ⚠	Repair/Adjust/ Replace	
4. Brake effort fluctuations while brakes are steadily applied	⚠ ⚠	Repair/Adjust/ Replace	
5. Severe grab or judder when brakes are applied	⚠ ⚠	Repair/Adjust/ Replace	

WARNING

 Extremely dangerous. DO NOT ride your motorcycle in this condition. You will be breaking the law and risking your life and the lives of others.

 Very dangerous. Put right immediately.

* Brake efficiency can only be measured with specialist equipment.

TYRES - 1

WHAT THE MOT REQUIRES	HOW TO CHECK YOUR TYRES
The Tyres The condition of ANY TYRE must not cause danger to any person on the motorcycle or on the road **You must not use your motorcycle on the road if ANY TYRE is unsuitable** • for the use to which you are putting the motorcycle, or • in relation to the tyres on the other wheel(s)	**Unsuitable tyres include** • sidecar tyres on a solo machine • motocross or similar tyres • tyres not designed for road use. For example, racing tyres or tyres marked NHS or NOT FOR HIGHWAY USE • a tyre designed for the front wheel and fitted to the rear wheel • a radial-ply tyre fitted to front wheel and a cross-ply tyre fitted to the rear • a bias-belted tyre fitted to the front wheel and a cross-ply tyre on the rear • a radial tyre on the front wheel and a bias-belted tyre on the rear

TYRES - 2

Are your tyres suitable ?

MAIN REASONS FOR FAILURE	REMARKS	ACTION	✓
1. Tyre is unsuitable		Replace	

WARNING

 Extremely dangerous. DO NOT ride your motorcycle in this condition.
You will be breaking the law and risking your life and the lives of others.

31

TYRES - 3

Are your tyres damaged ?

WHAT THE MOT REQUIRES	HOW TO CHECK YOUR TYRES
The Tyres **You must not use ANY TYRE that** 1. Has a cut • longer than 25mm, or 10% of the width of the tyre, whichever is the greater, and/or • deep enough to reach the ply 2. Has a lump, bulge or tear caused by the part failure of its structure 3. Has any exposed ply or cord 4. Has been recut	**How to check for wear and damage** a. Raise each wheel clear of the ground in turn b. Rotate each wheel slowly and check • seating of each tyre on the wheel rim • surface of the tyre, for damage/repairs etc c. Stop wheel and check valve stem for • cuts or other damage • alignment

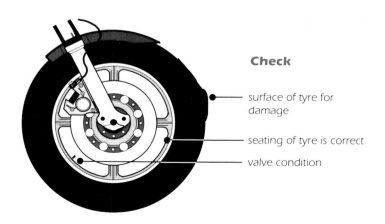

Check

surface of tyre for damage

seating of tyre is correct

valve condition

Are your tyres damaged ?

MAIN REASONS FOR FAILURE	REMARKS	ACTION	✓
1. A cut deep enough to reach ply or cord.	⚠ ⚠ ⚠	Replace	
2. A lump, bulge or tear caused by failure of its structure, such as • separation • lifting of thread	⚠ ⚠ ⚠	Replace	
3. Ply or cord exposed	⚠ ⚠ ⚠	Replace	
4. Valve stem • out of alignment • damaged, or • not fitting tightly	⚠ ⚠	Realign/ Replace if damaged	

WARNING

 Extremely dangerous. DO NOT ride your motorcycle in this condition. You will be breaking the law and risking your life and the lives of others.

 Very dangerous. Put right immediately.

TYRES - 5

Are you tyres worn below the legal limit ?

WHAT THE MOT REQUIRES	HOW TO CHECK YOUR TYRES
Tyre Tread **ON ANY TYRE** **1. Tread grooves** The base of any groove which showed in the original tread MUST be clearly seen (see 2b) **2. If your motorcycle has an engine capacity of more than 50cc** **a. Tread pattern** The grooves on the tread pattern of ALL TYRES must be not less than 1mm deep forming a continuous band at least THREE QUARTERS of the breadth of the tread and ALL THE WAY around **b. Depth of tread** The entire original tread must be visible with a continuous band ALL of the way around **3. If your motorcycle has an engine capacity of less than 50cc** the tread of the tyre may be less than 1mm IF the tread pattern can be clearly seen over the whole tread area	**How to look for wear and damage** a. Raise the wheels clear of the ground b. Rotate each wheel slowly and check ▪ tread wear ▪ seating of tyre on wheel ▪ direction of rotation marks on tyres (if any)

TREAD

PATTERN

A continous band at least 3/4 of the

breadth of the tread and ALL THE WAY

around the tyre

Are you tyres worn below the legal limit ?

MAIN REASONS FOR FAILURE	REMARK	ACTION	✓
1. Tread pattern is not clearly visible over whole tread area	⚠ ⚠ ⚠	Replace	
2. Less than 1mm of tread depth • around entire circumference, and • over at least three quarters of the width	⚠ ⚠	Replace	
3. A recut tread	⚠ ⚠ ⚠	Replace	
4. Tyre not correctly seated on wheel rim or, tubeless tyre not correctly seated	⚠ ⚠ ⚠ ⚠ ⚠	Refit correctly	
5. Tyre fitted to wrong direction of rotation (see instructions on sidewall)	⚠	Refit correctly	
6. Tyre rubbing against another part of the motorcycle	⚠ ⚠ ⚠	Repair/ Replace	

WARNING

 Extremely dangerous. DO NOT ride your motorcycle in this condition.

You will be breaking the law and risking your life and the lives of others.

 Very dangerous. Put right immediately.

 Could also be dangerous.

Tyre fitted in the correct

direction of rotation.

WHEELS - 1

Are your wheels in good condition ?

WHAT THE MOT REQUIRES	HOW TO CHECK YOUR WHEELS
The Wheels The condition of ANY WHEEL must not cause danger to any person on the motorcycle or on the road	**To look for wear and damage** a. Raise the wheels clear of the ground b. Spin the wheels and check for buckling and eccentricity c. Ensure no sideward movement is present between wheel and frame d. Check the condition and security of the wheel itself

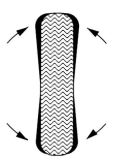

If the wheel is buckled or eccentric you will see the movement by rotating the wheel.

CRACKS OR OTHER DAMAGE could fail your bike.

Are your wheels in good condition ?

MAIN REASONS FOR FAILURE	REMARKS	ACTION	✓
1. Wheel is cracked or badly damaged	⚠️ ⚠️ ⚠️	Replace	
2. A spoke is missing, loose, bent, corroded, or cracked	⚠️	Tighten/Replace	
3. Loose or missing rivets or bolts in built-up wheels	⚠️ ⚠️ ⚠️	Tighten/Replace	
4. A cast light alloy wheel which has been repaired	⚠️ ⚠️	Replace	
5. The bead rim is distorted by more than a. 4mm for wire spoked wheels with steel or light alloy rims b. 2mm for cast light alloy wheel rims	⚠️ ⚠️	Replace/Repair *	
6. The eccentricity is more than 3mm	⚠️	Repair/Replace	
7. Loose or missing wheel nuts, studs or bolts	⚠️ ⚠️ ⚠️	Tighten/Replace	
8. An insecure wheel	⚠️ ⚠️ ⚠️	Tighten	

WARNING

 Extremely dangerous. DO NOT ride your motorcycle in this condition.

You will be breaking the law and risking your life and the lives of others.

 Very dangerous. Put right immediately.

 Could also be dangerous.

* Remember! A cast alloy wheel cannot usually be repaired satisfactorily. Seek expert advice

Damaged thread can make wheel nuts impossible to tighten. Replace nuts which won't stay tight.

SIDECAR - 1

Is the sidecar safe ?

WHAT THE MOT REQUIRES	HOW TO CHECK YOUR SIDECAR
The Sidecar The condition of the SIDECAR must not affect the stability of the motorcycle or cause danger to any person on the motorcycle or on the road	**How to check your sidecar is secure** Check the sidecar fixing devices are secure Try to move the sidecar on its own to make sure the attachment is secure For leanable sidecars check the operation of the attachment pivot joints

MAIN REASONS FOR FAILURE	REMARKS	ACTION	✓
1. Insecurity	⚠ ⚠ ⚠	Repair	
2. The attachment • has abnormal or excessive wear • is loose or insecure • is missing	⚠ ⚠ ⚠	Repair/Replace	
3. On a leanable sidecar the pivot points or bushes are • tight • excessively worn • extensively deteriorated	⚠ ⚠ ⚠	Repair/Replace	

WARNING

 Extremely dangerous. DO NOT ride your motorcycle in this condition.

You will be breaking the law and risking your life and the lives of others.

SIDECAR - 3

WHAT THE MOT REQUIRES	HOW TO CHECK YOUR SIDECAR
The Sidecar The condition of the SIDECAR must not affect the stability of the motorcycle or cause danger to any person on the motorcycle or on the road	**How to check the suspension on the sidecar is correct** a. Using your body weight, push down on the suspension as far as possible and check for • freedom of movement • security of unit b. Check for evidence of contact between fixed and moving parts c. Raise the sidecar wheel off the ground and check for • security • good condition of the wheel (see page 36) wheel bearings which must not be • excessively tight • rough • or have excessive free play

MAIN REASONS FOR FAILURE	REMARKS	ACTION	✓
1. Excessive stiffness suggesting partial seizure of suspension unit	⚠ ⚠	Replace	
2. An insecure suspension unit	⚠ ⚠	Tighten/Replace	
3. Loose or missing • wheel spindle • securing nuts • locking devices	⚠ ⚠ ⚠	Tighten/Replace	
4. Wheel bearings which • are excessively tight • have excessive free play • are rough whilst wheel is rotating	⚠	Adjust/Replace	

WARNING

 Extremely dangerous. DO NOT ride your motorcycle in this condition. You will be breaking the law and risking your life and the lives of others.

 Very dangerous. Put right immediately.

 Could also be dangerous.

SIDECAR - 5

Is the sidecar safe ?

WHAT THE MOT REQUIRES	HOW TO CHECK THE SIDECAR
The Sidecar The condition of the SIDECAR must not affect the stability of the motorcycle or cause danger to any person on the motorcycle or on the road	**How to check for wheel alignment on your sidecar** With the motorcycle combination on a flat surface and the steering straight ahead, check • there is no toe-out (pointing out) or too much toe-in (pointing in) of motorcycle and sidecar wheels • the vertical alignment of the motorcycle and sidecar

Is the sidecar safe ?

MAIN REASONS FOR FAILURE	REMARKS	ACTION	✓
1. The sidecar wheel relative to the motorcycle is • toed-in too much (pointing in) • toed-out (pointing out)	⚠	Adjust	
2. Wheel is too much out of vertical alignment	⚠	Adjust	

WARNING

⚠ Could be dangerous.

Parallel or slight toe-in

FRONT

REAR

✓

Any toe-out

FRONT

REAR

✗

Excessive toe-in

FRONT

REAR

✗

CORROSION - 1

Is your motorcycle sound and in good condition ?

WHAT THE MOT REQUIRES	HOW TO CHECK FOR CORROSION
Corrosion The effect of CORROSION must not affect the stability and safety of the motorcycle or cause danger to any person on the motorcycle or on the road	**The effect of corrosion on the safety of the motorcycle is not easy to assess** It depends on the extent of corrosion and on the function of the section on which it occurs For example, slight corrosion on important parts might be unsafe, while significant corrosion on a less important part might be acceptable The extent of corrosion can be assessed by pressing hard with • finger and thumb • shaft of hammer • any blunt instrument **but do not** • use a sharp instrument • use heavy blows When filler has been used to hide the corrosion it will emit a duller sound than metal when tapped To make sure your motorcycle passes there must be no excessive corrosion on the motorcycle and only very little on important structural parts of the motorcycle

CORROSION - 2

Is your motorcycle sound and in good condition ?

MAIN REASONS FOR FAILURE	REMARKS	ACTION	✓
1. Excessive corrosion	⚠ ⚠ ⚠	Replace part	
2. A corroded part not repaired with the correct materials and techniques	⚠ ⚠ ⚠	Replace	
3. If, under stress, the corrosion affects the safety of the motorcycle	⚠ ⚠ ⚠	Repair/Replace	
4. Load-bearing members or sections repaired using • pop rivetting • glass fibre	⚠ ⚠ ⚠	Replace	

WARNING

 Extremely dangerous. DO NOT ride your motorcycle in this condition.

You will be breaking the law and risking your life and the lives of others.

HORN - 1

WHAT THE MOT REQUIRES	HOW TO CHECK YOUR HORN
The Horn Your motorcycle must be fitted with a HORN capable of giving audible and sufficient warning of its approach or position If the motorcycle was registered after 1 August 1973 the sound must be continuous and uniform ONLY SPECIFIED motorcycles may be fitted with a • gong • bell • siren • two-tone horn (except as an anti-theft device)	**Check your motorcycle is fitted with the correct horn** Check the horn can easily be sounded Operate the horn and make sure it gives out the right sound

46

Is the correct horn fitted ?

MAIN REASONS FOR FAILURE	REMARKS	ACTION	✓
1. The horn is missing	⚠	Replace	
2. The horn is not working	⚠	Repair/Replace	
3. The horn is not loud enough	⚠	Repair/Replace	
4. The motorcycle is fitted with a • gong • bell • siren • two-tone horn	⚠	Repair/Replace	
5. The tone is not continuous or uniform	⚠	Repair/Replace	
6. The tone of the horn is harsh or grating	⚠	Repair/Replace	

WARNING

 Could be dangerous.

EXHAUST - 1

WHAT THE MOT REQUIRES	HOW TO CHECK YOUR EXHAUST
The Exhaust System Your motorcycle must be fitted with a SILENCER sufficient to reduce to a reasonable level the noise caused by the escape of the exhaust fumes from the engine If your motorcycle was registered after 1 January 1985, it must have a silencer that • is the one which was fitted from new OR • is permanently marked with either a. British Standards no. BSAU193, or b. a reference to its make and type specified by the manufacturer	**Check your motorcycle is fitted with the correct exhaust** When cold check the exhaust a. is secure b. has no holes c. has the correct identification plate (if applicable) With the engine running check the exhaust d. has no leaks letting out gas and noise

48

Is the correct exhaust fitted ?

MAIN REASONS FOR FAILURE	REMARKS	ACTION	✓
1. Any part of the exhaust system is missing or very deteriorated	⚠	Repair/Replace	
2. A leak causing excessive noise	⚠	Repair/Replace	
3. Any of the exhaust mountings are loose	⚠ ⚠	Tighten/Replace	
4. A silencer which is • in a bad condition • of a type that gives out excess noise	⚠	Replace	
5. A silencer fitted to a motorcycle first used after 1 January 1985 which is not • the one which was fitted from new • or permanently marked with either a. British Standards no. BSAU193, or b. a reference to its make and type specified by the manufacturer	⚠	Replace	
6. A silencer marked NOT FOR ROAD USE or with a similar warning	⚠	Replace	

WARNING

⚠ ⚠ Very dangerous. Put right immediately.

⚠ Could also be dangerous.

STRUCTURE - 1

WHAT THE MOT REQUIRES	HOW TO CHECK THE STRUCTURE
The Structure The STRUCTURE of your motorcycle must be sound and secure and must not cause danger to any person on the motorcycle or on the road	**Check that your motorcycle is in a good structural condition** Check a. the frame b. the seat and foot rest c. the transmission component (chain/belt) and chain guard

Is the structure of your motorcycle safe ?

MAIN REASONS FOR FAILURE	REMARKS	ACTION	✓
1. A part of the motorcycle is • cracked • damaged • distorted • corroded and is likely to affect the functioning of the steering or brakes	⚠ ⚠ ⚠	Repair/Replace	
2. A loose or unsafe seat or footrest	⚠ ⚠	Repair/Replace	
3. A fault which is likely to prevent the rear wheel rotating such as a loose or faulty chain/belt/drive shaft	⚠ ⚠ ⚠	Tighten/Replace	

WARNING

 Extremely dangerous. DO NOT ride your motorcycle in this condition.

You will be breaking the law and risking your life and the lives of others.

 Very dangerous. Put right immediately.

IF YOUR MOTORCYCLE FAILS

If your motorcycle has failed the test,
please read the following notes

1. Your motorcycle does not meet the legal requirements. If you intend to continue to use it on the road, you should have it repaired WITHOUT DELAY.

2. You will be committing an offence if you use the motorcycle on the road if it does not have a current test certificate, except when

- it is not of a testable age, or when you are
- taking it to a testing station for a test BOOKED IN ADVANCE
- bringing it away from a testing station after it has failed the test
- taking it to (or from) a place where by PREVIOUS ARRANGEMENT repairs are to be done to remedy the defects for which the motorcycle was failed.

Even in these circumstances, you can still be prosecuted if the motorcycle is not roadworthy under the various regulations affecting its construction and use. Also, the insurance may not cover you to ride the motorcycle.

HOW TO APPEAL

If your motorcycle fails its MOT Test, you may if you wish appeal to the Vehicle Inspectorate's District Office using form VT17. The MOT Testing station is bound by law to give you the address of the office and copies of the form.

A fee is payable which is given back if your appeal succeeds. The completed form (the notice of appeal) and fee must be received by the Vehicle Inspectorate's District Office within 14 days of the test.

DO NOT repair or alter the items which are the subject of your appeal before the Inspectorate has examined them. If you do repair or alter them the outcome of the appeal may be affected.

Printed in the United Kingdom for HMSO
Dd 291873   C50   3/90